BRANCH LINE TO LYME REGIS

Vic Mitchell and Keith Smith

"The branch had a rare charm about it, it traversed picturesque country-side and its vintage motive power remained unchanged for more than forty years." – R.C. Riley

Cover: *Adams Radial 4 – 4 – 2T no. 30582 leaves Axminster for Lyme Regis at 12.33 on 3rd July 1958. (J Scrace)*

Design – Deborah Goodridge

First published August 1987

ISBN 0 906520 45 2

© *Middleton Press, 1987*

Typeset by CitySet - Bosham 573270

Published by Middleton Press
      Easebourne Lane
      Midhurst, West Sussex
      GU29 9AZ
      ☎ *073 081 3169*

Printed & bound by Biddles Ltd,
      Guildford and Kings Lynn

CONTENTS

ACKNOWLEDGEMENTS

We are grateful for the help received from Mrs. E. Fisk, Mrs. S. Grove, Lyme Regis (Philpot) Museum, R. Randell, N. Stanyon and our wives.

The photographs of the late E. Wallis are reproduced by permission of Mrs. M. Mason and Mr. D. Wallis.

Our thanks also goes to N. Langridge and G. Croughton for providing tickets from their collections.

GEOGRAPHICAL SETTING

Axminster is situated near the confluences of the Rivers Yarty and Axe, the latter arising south of Crewkerne. Whilst the main line west follows the Axe Valley, the branch immediately climbs the side of the valley, crossing two small tributaries of the Axe. Many of the gradients are at 1 in 40, the summit being reached near Combpyne.

The geology of the area is extremely varied, giving rise to the pleasant undulating landform and problems for the railway constructors. The deposits include upper greensand, chalk and a variety of clays giving unstable cuttings.

At Combpyne the route changes from a north-south axis to an east-west one and enters the valley of one of the headwaters of the River Lim. After crossing it on a substantial viaduct, the line runs high on the side of the valley to the terminus 250ft, above sea level.

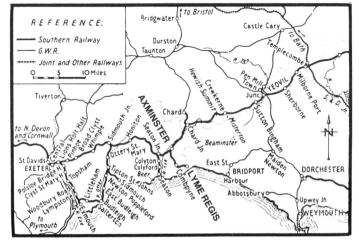

Pre-nationalisation map of the
surrounding district. (Railway Magazine)

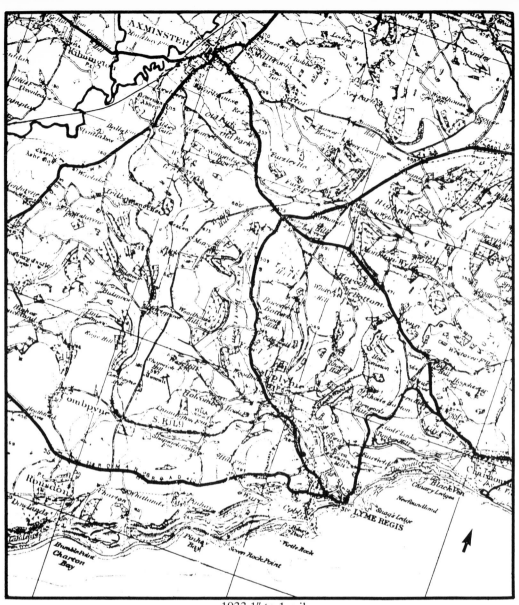

1933 1" to 1 mile

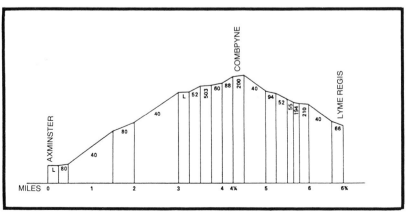

HISTORICAL BACKGROUND

A small harbour at Lyme Regis was in being in the 14th century but by the 17th century ships has become too big for it. The village went into decline until the early 19th century when it began to develop as a holiday resort for the wealthy few able to enjoy any leisure time. Early tourism was given a boost with the development of a popular interest in geology and palaeontology in the "educated classes."

In the "Railway Mania" of the 1840's, a Somerset and Dorset Railway was proposed, linking Bridgwater with Lyme Regis, but it was not until after the passing of the Light Railway Act in 1896 that the resort was to hear of a successful scheme.

A light Railway Order was made in 1899 and Mr. Arthur C. Pain was appointed Engineer. He was also involved with the Southwold Railway and the Culm Valley line.

The route was opened on 24th August 1903 and the London & South Western Railway's financial involvement with the company resulted in the former receiving 55% of the revenue. Owing to its poor financial results, the company was taken over entirely by the LSWR on 1st January 1907. At about this time, conventional signalling was installed and by 1912 all the original lightweight flat-bottomed rail had been replaced.

The line became part of the Southern Railway on 1st January 1923 and in 1948, part of the Southern Region of British Railways, later being transferred to the Western Region.

Little changed on the branch until goods services were withdrawn on 3rd February 1964 and, after a period of diesel operation, passenger services ceased on 29th November 1965.

PASSENGER SERVICES

Weekday branch services

The Axminster & Lyme Regis Light Railway offered six return journeys, although services were operated by the LSWR. When the latter took control in 1907, the frequency was increased to eight. An unexpected boost to traffic in 1908 was caused by a geological fault. A massive landslip took place in the cliffs south of Combpyne and the ground caught fire, burning spectacularly for eight months.

The SR steadily increased the service until the summer 1938 timetable showed eleven trains. With a curtailment of road transport during WWII rail services were usually maintained – nine journeys being typical in 1942. Thereafter ten was the usual figure until 1951, with extras on Saturdays. Nine trips per day were made from then until closure.

Sunday branch services

None were provided until 1930. During the 1930's the summer frequency ranged from 6 to 11. A regular, if sparse, service was maintained during WWII and until the winter of 1950 – 51. Thereafter the winter timetable showed the local bus times, which omitted Combpyne. The summer service ranged from eight to eleven trips each way.

Through services

Through coaches to and from Waterloo were run in the summer timetables from June 1953 until September 1963. Until 1959, there was one return service on Monday to Fridays with two on Saturdays. Thereafter they ran on Saturdays only, with an unbalanced two up and one down service. Although not a direct part of the much-divided "Atlantic Coast Express", some of the branch coaches did become part of it, east of Salisbury.

THE LYME VOLCANO

The spectacular burning landscape was thus described at the time, although incorrectly. The combustion was due to the rapid oxidation of iron pyrites following rapid earth movement. This in turn caused a conflagration of the pyrolitic shales, which contain varying amounts of oil. A small area was eventually used as a convenient means of disposal of domestic rubbish.

LOCOMOTIVES

Original class	Original owner	Wheel arrangement	Main period of use	Typical numbers
330	Contractor	0–6–0ST	1900-03	131
A1	LBSCR	0–6–0T	1903-07	734, 735
02	LSWR	0–4–4T	1906-13	177, 202, 227, 228
415	LSWR	4–4–2T	1913-61	30582, 30583, 30584
2MT	LMS	2–6–2T	1960-63	41291, 297, 308, 318

The above table is a summary of the successful and moderately successful locomotives used on this unique stiffly graded and sharply curved branch. In the latter category is the A1 'Terrier' class, due to its limited power, and the 02 class. These regularly had twisted frames, worn wheels and, moreover, had to run with tanks half full to avoid exceeding the limited axle weight of 12 tons.

In the late 1920's ex-LBSCR class D1 0–4–2Ts and an ex-SECR P class 0–6–0T were tried but they could not match the ex-LWSR 415 class 4–4–2Ts, which had been designed by Adams in the 1880's and were nicknamed the "Radials" due to their unusual bogie linkage.

With the increasing age of the Radials, alternatives were sought and trials of an ex-GWR 0–4–2T and a BR class 2 2–6–2T were carried out and are illustrated in this album, at several locations.

Regular usage of steam ceased in November 1963 and the branch was thereafter worked by two-coach diesel multiple units, which were largely superseded by single railcars in March 1965.

1. No. 734 and 735 worked the branch in its early years. They were formerly LBSCR no. 46 *Newington* and no. 68 *Clapham* and had been members of a large class of successful tanks working hard on mainly South London suburban services.
(E. R. Lacey collection)

Summary of the later Radial tanks

BR number	SR number	LSWR number	Builder	Disposal
30582	3125	125	Stephenson	Scrapped 1962
30583	3488	488	Neilson	Bluebell Rly.
30584	3520	520	Dübs & Co	Scrapped 1961

2. Typical of the LSWR 415 class, which gave nearly 50 years of service on the branch, is no. 30582, seen outside Exmouth Junction shed on 15th July 1960 after a works visit. These Radials proved to be ideal for the unusual conditions of the Lyme Regis route. (R.C. Riley)

3. Now preserved on the Bluebell Railway, this locomotive served the LSWR as no. 488 until 1917 when acquired by the Ministry of Munitions. It became East Kent Railway no. 5 in 1919 and when the SR became desperate in 1946 for an engine to relieve its two remaining Radials, this engine was bought for £800. An extensive rebuild at Eastleigh gave a trio for the Lyme Regis branch and a unique engine for the Bluebell Railway to rebuild, yet again, in 1971-72. (S.W. Baker)

This table gives a summary of the three Radial tanks that were the mainstay of branch motive power for over 30 years, although no. 3488 did not arrive until 1946. A few other members of the class ran on the branch in the 1920s. All three locomotives were built in 1885, although by different firms. The original Adams designed boilers are evident by the safety valve cover being placed close to the cab and the dome cover being large and smooth. The later Drummond designed boilers had two safety valves projecting through a smaller dome cover.

AXMINSTER

4. The station opened, with the main line, on 19th July 1860. The buildings were designed by Sir William Tite and still display a stone engraved "1859". A horse bus ran twice a day to Lyme Regis from about 1880, being operated by Mr. John Groves of the Royal Lion Hotel in Lyme Regis. (Lens of Sutton)

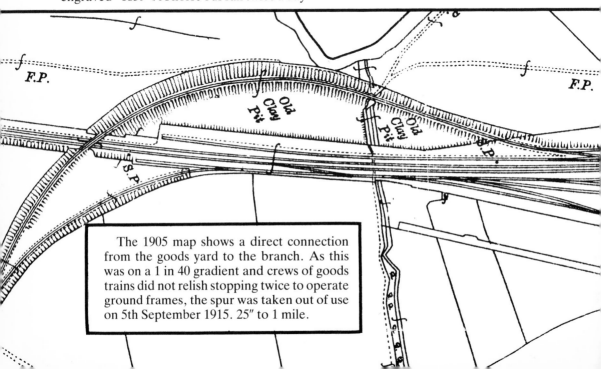

The 1905 map shows a direct connection from the goods yard to the branch. As this was on a 1 in 40 gradient and crews of goods trains did not relish stopping twice to operate ground frames, the spur was taken out of use on 5th September 1915. 25″ to 1 mile.

5. A westward view from the footbridge in September 1928 shows the branch line curving away from its bay on the right and crossing the bridge over the main line, in the distance. Unfortunately, the glass slide has been damaged. (Late E. Wallis)

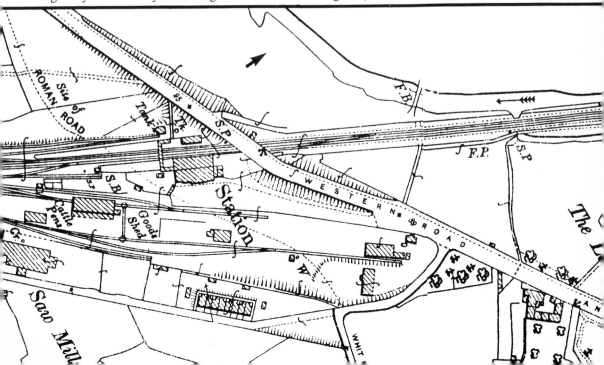

6. A photograph from September 1929 shows no. 0520 with its maximum load of three coaches. The SR added the prefix E to the Eastleigh or ex-LSWR engines. The horse boxes in the dock siding remind us of this once important traffic. (Dr. I.C. Allen)

7. No. 3125 drifts into the bay platform with coach set no. 36, sporting its new Southern fully lined livery. The SR eventually gave the prefix 3 to the LSWR numbers, instead of E. (Lens of Sutton)

8. Sister engine, no. 3520, was similarly renumbered and repainted in the Southern's smart passenger engine green. This view also shows the catch points in the run round loop. (D. Cullum collection)

9. This 1934 view was taken from a departing train and shows passengers from it joining the branch service, while the driver benefits from the spacious running plates during oiling up. (Dr. I.C. Allen)

←

10. The branch engine returned to Exmouth Junction shed every Saturday for boiler washout and routine maintenance, the other engine of the pair allocated to the line having arrived earlier in the day. No. 30584 is seen on 26th June 1949, attached to class S15 no. 30845 which heads a train bound for Barnstaple. (S.C. Nash)

11. No. 30584 (nee 3520 before its marriage numerically to its two sisters by BR) starts the climb over the main line on 18th June 1949. The train appears to carry a guard although one was not required for trains of under three coaches for many years. (S.C. Nash)

AXMINSTER and LYME REGIS May 1948

Miles	Down	Week Days																					
		B	S O	S O		S X	S O	S X		S O	S X	S O	S X		S X	S O	p.m	p.m	p.m		p.m		p.m
	Axminster .... dep	8 35	9 30	1030	..	1043	1130	12 2	..	1230	1257	1 30	1 53	..	2 50	3 20	4 40	5 40	6 50	..	8 55	..	9 J ‖ 45
4¼	Combpyne	8 47	9 42	1042	..	1055	1142	1214	..	1242	1 9	1 42	2 5	..	3 2	3 32	4 52	5 52	7 2	..	9 7	..	..
6¾	Lyme Regis .... arr	8 56	9 51	1051	..	11 4	1151	1223	..	1251	1 18	1 51	2 14	..	3 11	4 41	5 1	6 1	7 11	..	9 16	..	10 J ‖ 11

Miles	Up	Week Days																					
		a.m	K	S O		a.m		S O		S X	S O		S X	S O		S X	S X	S O		p.m	p.m	p.m	p.m
	Lyme Regis .... dep	7 J 20	8 4	9 0	..	10 0	..	11 0	..	1134	12 0	..	1229	1 0	..	1 24	2 19	2 45	..	3 55	5 10	6 7	8 20
2¼	Combpyne	..	8 12	9 8	..	10 8	..	11 8	..	1142	12 8	..	1237	1 8	..	1 32	2 27	2 53	..	4 3	5 18	6 15	8 28
6¾	Axminster 340, 347 ... arr	7 J 49	8 25	9 21	..	10 21	..	1121	..	1155	1221	..	1250	1 21	..	1 45	2 40	3 6	..	4 16	5 31	6 28	8 41

Down	Sundays							Up	Sundays							
	a.m	p.m	p.m	p.m	p.m	p.m	p.m		a.m	a.m	p.m	p.m	p.m	p.m	p.m	
Axminster .... dep	1111	1240	3 10	4 20	5 50	7 33	8 30	Lyme Regis .... dep	1040	1137	2 35	3 50	5 10	7 0	7 56	..
Combpyne	1123	1252	3 22	4 32	6 2	7 45	8 42	Combpyne	1048	1145	2 43	3 58	5 18	7 8	8 6	..
Lyme Regis .... arr	1132	1 1	3 31	4 41	6 11	7 54	8 51	Axminster 340, 347 .... arr	11 1	1158	2 56	4 11	5 31	7 21	8 19	..

B Runs 3 minutes *earlier* on Saturdays. J By Southern National Omnibus. Times subject to alteration.
K Runs 4 mins. *earlier* on Saturdays. ‖ Commences 4th June. S O Saturdays only. S X Saturdays excepted.

12. "Dropping off the pilot". An up train stands on the embankment approaching the station on 18th August 1951, as the pilot engine runs past the branch home signal, the "dolly" at the bottom of the post "off" for it. The train will soon be free to run into the bay. (S.W. Baker)

13. Battle of Britain class no. 34050 heads west on 18th August 1951, while the branch engine couples onto the front of a westbound goods train so that it can return to its home shed no. 72A, confirmed on its smokebox door. (S.W. Baker)

14. Through coaches from Waterloo to Lyme Regis were detached and collected from the down platform by the branch engine. No. 30583 approaches the single coach on 9th September 1953, as the shunter signals from the up line. (S.W. Baker)

15. A few minutes later, we see the assemblage emerge from the confines of the road bridge, bound for the up siding. It will wait there and then reverse onto the branch coaches, waiting in the bay. (S.W. Baker)

16. In the summer of 1954, the Waterloo train was longer and so the through coach was left further down the platform extension. The shunter stands with one hand on the coach, as passengers stretch their legs in this interlude towards the end of their long journey. (S.W. Baker)

17. On 28th June 1953, an unusual enthusiasts' train ran to celebrate the 25th anniversary of the RCTS. The pilot engine is familiar on the branch but the train engine is ex-LBSCR "Terrier" no. 32662. (P. Hay)

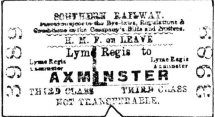

SOUTHERN RAILWAY.
H. M. F. on LEAVE
Lyme Regis to
AXMINSTER
THIRD CLASS   THIRD CLASS
NOT TRANSFERABLE.

18. The special train is seen climbing the 1 in 80 gradient to the bridge over the main line, from the abutment of which this photograph was taken. No. 32662 was withdrawn ten years later and is now to be found in Bressingham Museum. (P. Hay)

19. No. 30583 simmers outside the carpet factory on 19th June 1954, as class S15 no. 30830 proceeds west with a semi-fast. The factory had been founded by Thomas Witty in 1755 and despatched up to five rail vans per day in the 1950s, loaded with carpets for various destinations. (S.W. Baker)

20. A July 1956 photograph shows a horse box in the same position as that in the one taken nearly 30 years earlier. Also visible in the goods yard is the 1½-ton capacity fixed crane and an Esso tank wagon. The locomotive is just about to run round the coaches. (R.C. Riley)

21. The shining black BR livery, bearing the rampant lion, is how many will remember these fine veteran locomotives. No. 30584 approaches the branch up home on 10th July 1956. This signal was removed in 1960, after which the branch was worked "one engine in steam". (R.C. Riley)

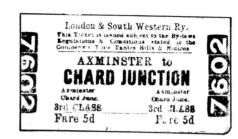

London & South Western Ry.

This Ticket is issued subject to the By-laws Regulations & Conditions stated in the Company's Time Tables Bills & Notices

AXMINSTER to

CHARD JUNCTION

Axminster	Axminster
Chard June.	Chard June.
3rd CLASS	3rd CLASS
Fare 5d	Fare 5d

22. Six coaches was the limit for scheduled trains on account of platform length. This "special" of Midland Region coaches ran annually for the Oldham Boys' Brigade and remained in a siding at Lyme for the week's duration of the camp. It is seen returning on 27th June 1959. (S.C. Nash)

23. An April shower in 1960 reminds us that whilst the footbridge was fully roofed the up platform was always devoid of a canopy. Both passengers are having to walk the length of the platform as the driver did not first take the train up to the buffers before reversing back for water. (A.E. Bennett)

24. The branch engine could conveniently take water at the up platform between other duties and returning to its coaches in the bay. The generous shelter and passenger facilities on the down side compare notably with the mean shelter on the up, as shown in this 1960 view. (E. Wilmshurst)

25. This 1960 photograph is included to show the water column, the coal stage, the water tank and the massive chimney that for many years served a steam engine used to power a pump. Water was pumped from the nearby River Axe. (S.W. Baker)

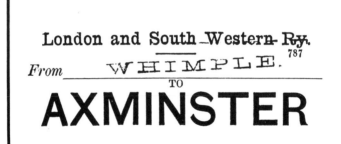

London and South Western Ry.

From _____ WHIMPLE. 787

TO

AXMINSTER

26. The driver stands with his hand on the wheel valve while the fireman stands in the bunker to retain the bag in the filler. Other details to note are the coal wagon at the end of the line and the two-lever ground frame, in use in 1960. (C.L. Caddy)

27. The branch locomotive had to first enter the up platform to gain access to the goods yard or the down platform. Leaning against the seat is one of the folding covers that were supposed to be fitted to the corridor gangway at the end of the train.
(E. Wilmshurst)

28. Four more views from 1960 complete our story of the Adams Radial era here. No. 30583, now on the Bluebell Railway, brings a single through coach into the up sidings, having shunted it over the trailing crossovers between the main lines.
(E. Wilmshurst)

29. It stands in the up siding awaiting the arrival of the 11.08 from Lyme Regis, behind no. 30584. This will then run round while no. 30583 propels the single coach on to the other two, ready to leave at 11.39.
(E. Wilmshurst)

30. The 10.45 from Waterloo arrived at 1.39 and left these coaches for no. 30583 to take forward to Lyme Regis from the bay at 1.55. The wooden path in the foreground linked the down platform with the barrow crossing. (J.H. Aston)

31. Superb views westwards, over the Axe valley and beyond, were to be had as the train gently descended the sharply curved embankment. The hexagonal structure was one of a number erected in this vicinity in the early part of World War II as a defence in the event of invasion. The slit for a gun can be seen. They were called "pill boxes" and a number still stand in this locality. (J.H. Aston)

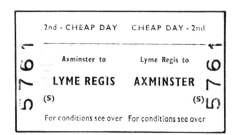

32. The new motive power is seen in use on 8th August 1961 but the coaches are ageing pre-war Maunsell ones. The up siding and the short one branching from it were used by the Permanent Way department. (Dr. T.A. Gough)

33. In the latter years of steam, it appears that the coaches as well as the locomotives changed over each Saturday and returned to Exmouth Junction. Here no. 41321 comes on duty, whilst behind it and its two coaches No. 42191 waits to be relieved, on 31st May 1963. (J.H. Aston)

34. No. 42191 is seen later the same day, having run round its train and pushed it up to the stops so that passengers did not have too far to walk from the footbridge. It waits to depart at 6.47 pm. (J.H. Aston)

35. Two-car diesel multiple units were first used on the branch in November 1963, but by the time this photograph was taken on 13th March 1965, a single car sufficed. Only the down side structures now remain.
(C.L. Caddy)

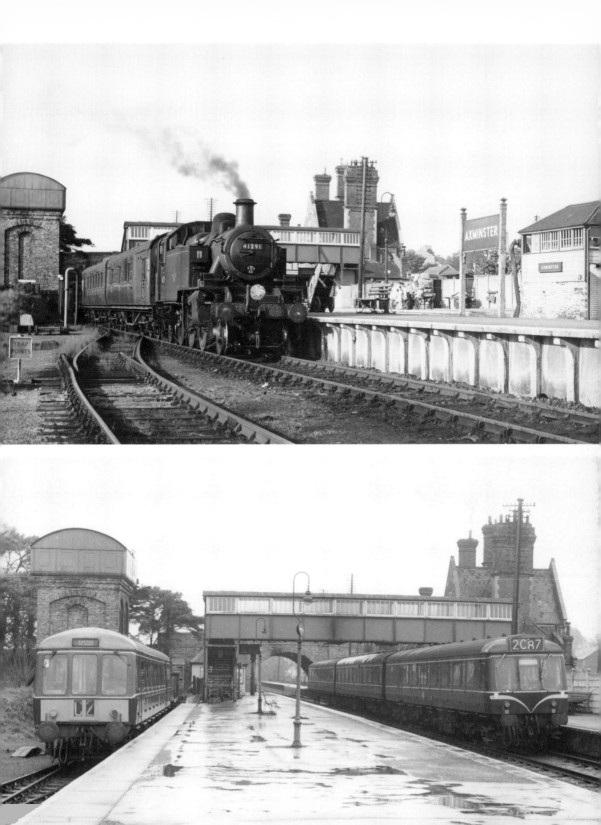

36. Railcar no. W55000 waits in the bay on 12th April 1965 whilst "Warship" class diesel-hydraulic no. D823 *Hermes* heads an Exeter service. The signal box and the down sidings ceased to be used after 5th March 1967 and the main line was singled on 11th June 1967. (D. Fereday Glenn)

AXMINSTER and LYME REGIS
Second class only

June 1964

Miles		Mondays to Fridays											Saturdays				
		am		am		am		pm	pm	pm	pm	pm	pm		pm	am	am	am	am	pm	pm
	Axminster .. .. dep	7 15	..	8 8	..	1015	..	1230	1 42	2 45	4 35	5 40	6 40	..	10Y 5	..	7 15	8 10	1035	11 27	1215	1 25
4¼	Combpyne	7 26	..	8 20	..	1026	..	1241	1 53	2 56	4 46	5 51	6 51	..	..	..	7 26	8 21	1046	11 39	1227	1 36
6¾	Lyme Regis .. .. arr	7 33	..	8 26	..	1033	..	1248	2 0	3 3	4 53	5 58	6 58	..	10Y32	..	7 33	8 28	1053	11 45	1233	1 45

	Saturdays—continued							Sundays							
		pm	pm	pm	pm	pm		pm		am		pm	pm	pm	pm	pm		pm	pm	pm
Axminster .. .. dep	2 25	3 40	4 35	5 40	6 50	..	10Y 5	..	11 6	..	1210	1 2	2 10	3 15	4 30	..	5 48	7 16	8 25	..	..	..
Combpyne	2 37	3 51	4 46	5 51	7 1	..	..	..	1117	..	1221	1 13	2 21	3 26	4 41	..	5 59	7 27	8 36	..	..	..
Lyme Regis .. .. arr	2 43	3 58	4 53	5 58	7 8	..	10Y32	..	1124	..	1228	1 20	2 28	3 33	4 48	..	6 6	7 34	8 43	..	..	..

Miles		Mondays to Fridays													Saturdays			
		am		am	am	am	am	pm	pm	pm	pm	pm		am	am		am		pm
	Lyme Regis .. .. dep	6Y31	..	7 38	9 45	11 32	1 10	2 9	4 5	5 13	6 10	7 2	..	6Y31	7 38	..	9 45	11 0	..	1150	..	12 40
2½	Combpyne	..	..	7 44	9 52	11 38	1 17	2 15	4 11	5 20	6 16	7 9	..	..	7 45	..	9 52	11 7	..	1156	..	12 46
6¾	Axminster .. .. arr	6Y58	..	7 56	10 3	11 50	1 30	2 27	4 23	5 31	6 28	7 20	..	6Y58	7 56	..	10 8	11 18	..	12 8	..	12 56

	Saturdays—continued								Sundays						
		pm	pm	pm	pm	pm	pm			am		pm	pm	pm	pm	pm		pm	pm		pm
Lyme Regis .. .. dep	1 48	2 50	4 25	5 15	6 10	7 25	..	..	1137	..	1231	1 40	2 45	4 0	5 13	..	6 40	7 45	..	8 50	..	..
Combpyne	1 56	2 56	4 8	5 21	6 16	7 31	..	..	1144	..	1238	1 47	2 52	4 7	5 20	..	6 47	7 52	..	8 57	..	..
Axminster .. .. arr	2 6	3 8	4 20	5 33	6 28	7 43	..	..	1155	..	1249	1 58	3 4	4 18	5 31	..	6 58	8 3	..	9 8	..	..

Y By Southern National Omnibus between Axminster Station and Lyme Regis. Times subject to alteration

SOUTH OF AXMINSTER

37. We include a greater number of inter-
mediate photographs than usual in this
album to emphasise the beauty of the
countryside and the added charm of a branch
train in it. No. 30584 gets to grips with the
steep gradient on 3rd August 1959 followed
by a BR standard non-corridor compartment
2nd; an ex-SECR 10-compartment non-
corridor 2nd and a Maunsell corridor brake
composite. (D. Fereday Glenn)

38. About two miles from Axminster, the line winds through an area known as Trill. On 27th June 1959, nos 30582 and 30583 were to be found struggling with the through coaches from Waterloo – a smart set of Bulleid's design. (S.C. Nash)

39. The severity of the curves is indicated by the crow's flight path taken by the telephone wires. The same two engines creak round the curves as they brake the Waterloo-bound coaches in September 1960. (S.C. Nash)

40. Apart from an occupation bridge near Trill, there was only one overbridge on this section of the route and it carried a public highway near Hartgrove Farm. The 6.50 pm from Axminster passes under it, on 1st August 1959. (D. Fereday Glenn)

41. Youthful holidaymakers enjoy the country air (and the aroma of hot cylinder oil, perhaps) having just passed Hartgrove Farm on 7th May 1960. The viscosity of the oil was improved by keeping it close to the smokebox. (D. Fereday Glenn)

42. The class 2 2–6–2Ts made light work of the 1 in 40 gradient. Witness *five* coaches being hauled unassisted on 29th July 1961. Milepost 3 was nearby and so was a short level length of track, but this was barely noticeable to loco crews. (D. Fereday Glenn)

43. On the same day, the same locomotive is seen producing the ideal clear exhaust. The elimination of double heading at times of peak summer traffic brought some saving in operational costs, but insufficient to save the line. (D. Fereday Glenn)

44. The line was bounded by woodland north of Combpyne and on the other side of the track were the steep slopes of Edge Hill. Where better to wait to photograph the 5.10pm from Lyme on Whit Monday in 1960. (S.C. Nash)

45. Nos. 30584 and '83 are seen returning about 30 minutes later, with the 5.40pm from Axminster. A superb Devonshire panorama stretches into the distance. (S.C. Nash)

COMBPYNE

46. Like Lyme Regis, Combpyne was supplied with a 14-lever signal box but only four of them were used. Two loop lines ran round the other side of the platform and very short sidings ran off both ends of one. This rare view of the box was taken in September 1928. (Late E. Wallis)

47. In 1930 the signal box was removed, being sold to nearby Hook Farm for agricultural purposes. The northern points were also taken away, converting the loop into a long siding. A new platform face was erected from concrete slabs, the other one being formed into a gently sloping bank.
(Lens of Sutton)

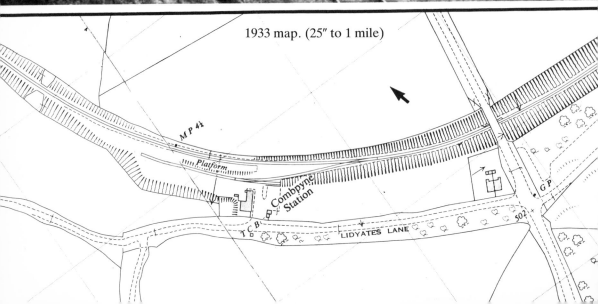

1933 map. (25″ to 1 mile)

48. A photograph from 18th June 1949 shows no. 30584 in the early BR plain lettering which was quite transitory. The materials in the foreground could be used by either Permanent Way gang as the station was their common boundary. (S.C. Nash)

49. An ex-LCDR coach was provided for letting to holiday makers. It would have suited hikers well, as there were no other leisure activities in the district. No. 30583 arrives from Axminster on 13th September 1950. (S.W. Baker)

50. As the gradient post indicates, the incline eases into the station, the summit being a little further east. The widening of the formation in the foreground of this 1957 photograph indicates the site of the former western points of the loop. (P. Hay)

51. The peace of this delightful location was occasionally disturbed by the shunting in of a van of bagged fertiliser or the shunting out of some agricultural products. Mixed trains were permitted, as witnessed here on 23rd July 1958. (R.C. Riley)

52. The trial run of ex-GWR 0-4-2T no. 1462 was recorded on 12th November 1958. These locomotives were hugely successful on branch lines over a wide area, but the curves to Lyme beat them! (S.C. Nash)

53. The later camping coach was more spacious but was still devoid of any services and heating. It returned to Eastleigh each winter for maintenance and is unusual in being fitted with a wagon-type handbrake. (J.H. Aston)

54. The single storey station office and the station house were remarkably remote from the platform. Both survive, in use as a dwelling. The small cattle dock is also visible in this photograph of no. 30584 on 8th July 1959. Few people walked the ¾ mile uphill from the small village, so passenger traffic was minimal. (R.C. Riley)

55. An unusual event took place on 18th September 1960, when class 2 2–6–2T no. 41297 arrived on the branch to undertake clearance tests. Some track relaying took place prior to the regular operation of this class – evidence is on the right. (S.C. Nash)

In 1970, Minirail Ltd commenced laying a 10¼″ gauge railway northwards from Combpyne. There were 13 coaches from Longleat and a Curzon locomotive but capital was exhausted by 1972 and a fare paying passenger was never carried. The coaches were converted in 1978 to 15″ gauge and given battery power to run at Blaise Castle, near Bristol.

56. Most freight was conveyed on the first train of the day, which was goods only. Wagons from Combpyne destined for the main line were routed via Lyme Regis. The churns conveyed domestic water from Lyme as the well ran dry in summer – during one such condition it was accidentally filled with rubbish and the churns were used permanently thereafter. (Lens of Sutton)

By March 1987, few would realise that this desirable residence was formerly part of a railway station. The only clue is a curb formed from a running rail. (V. Mitchell)

EAST OF COMBPYNE

57. East of the station, the line passes under the Rousdon to Axminster road, a "ridge-way" with excellent views. We see no. 30584 on 2nd August 1959, running bunker first as usual, the square spectacles being particularly evident. (D. Fereday Glenn)

58. No. 3125, later 30582, gleams with even her wheelspokes spotless as she hauls a mixed train. Next to the engine is a road van, fitted with side doors for the loading of parcels. (D. Cullum collection)

59. No. 30582 adds interest to the landscape on 12th August 1960, as she runs near Shapwick Grange Farm. A branch of the Cannington Valley reaches to within ½ mile of the coast and the main valley runs north before curving south to the sea. It is this unusual phenomena that necessitated the construction of a viaduct. (J.H. Aston)

CANNINGTON VIADUCT

60. This was one of the earliest examples of a major concrete construction in the South of England. 'Concrete Bob' McAlpine had just successfully completed an even more impressive series of bridges and viaducts on the Inverness-Mallaig line.
(A.H. Brown collection)

61. Shortly after construction, pier no.1 and the west abutment settled vertically due to the sandy foundations not accepting the design load of 3 tons per sq.ft. This view shows the formwork still in place in the second and fourth arches, prior to the erection of diaphragm walls or a jack arch in the third. (British Rail)

62. The use of concrete avoided the expense of scaffolding, as all materials could be conveyed by a 1000ft. long cableway supported by two wooden pylons, one of which is visible on the left. Mass concrete was employed, with the exception of concrete blocks in the exteriors of the piers and arches. Some were left projecting as corbels to support the arch centering. (A.H. Brown collection)

63. The settlement at the west end is evident as no.30584 clatters towards Axminster in its early BR livery on 18th June 1949. The concrete was made from flints, crushed after removal from the chalk excavated from nearby cuttings. (S.C. Nash)

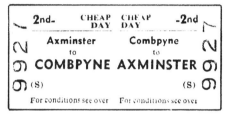

64. A bowler-hatted inspector gazes at the well-informed cameraman as ex-GWR no. 1462 makes its only revenue earning trip on the branch, on 12th November 1958. (S.C. Nash)

65. The jack arch upsets the symmetrical appearance of the structure but the beauty of the valley is tarnished little. The undisturbed serenity of the location was captured on 2nd June 1959, as the 11.37 from Lyme Regis climbed at the regulation 25 mph over the arches. (J.H. Aston)

67. The two local and four through coaches help to show that the track formation was built up to partly compensate for the settlement. A flagman was posted at each end of the viaduct to keep watch on its stability but there has been no movement reported in the subsequent 80 years. The LSWR withdrew this unnecessary precaution when they took control of the line. (Dr. I.C. Allen)

66. Another tranquil scene was captured on the same day, from the east side of the valley. The 10 o'clock from Lyme grinds round the sharp curve approaching this unusual switch-back construction. (S.C. Nash)

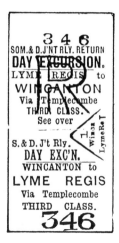

346
SOM.& D.J'NT RLY. RETURN
DAY EXCURSION.
LYME REGIS to
WINCANTON
Via Templecombe
THIRD CLASS.
See over

S. & D. J't Rly.
DAY EXC'N.
WINCANTON to
LYME REGIS
Via Templecombe
THIRD CLASS.
346

68. No. 41297 hauls the 12.00 special train from Lyme Regis on 18th September 1960, the first day a class 2 was tried on the branch. No one watched the viaduct and it appears as sturdy as ever, although there is a little spalling of the rendering of the small area of brickwork, used to repair the settlement damage nearly 90 years ago. Despite this, plans are being made to demolish this piece of local history. (S.C. Nash)

69. No station has ever been provided here although surprise has sometimes been expressed at the omission. The gradient here is 1 in 40 towards the sea – one would have not been possible at half that. No. 30582 is seen bound for Axminster on 14th June 1949. (S.C. Nash)

70. She is seen returning the same day, passing under a lane which is steeper than 1 in 7. The deep cuttings were prone to blockage by drifting snow and in the severe winter of 1962-63 a locomotive often ran all night to keep them clear. (S.C. Nash)

LYME REGIS (LSWR)

71. Considerable ceremony was attached to the opening of the line on 24th August 1903, the first train being hauled by Terriers nos. 734 and 735. We make no apology for repeating these well known and worthwhile photographs of the event. (A.H. Brown collection)

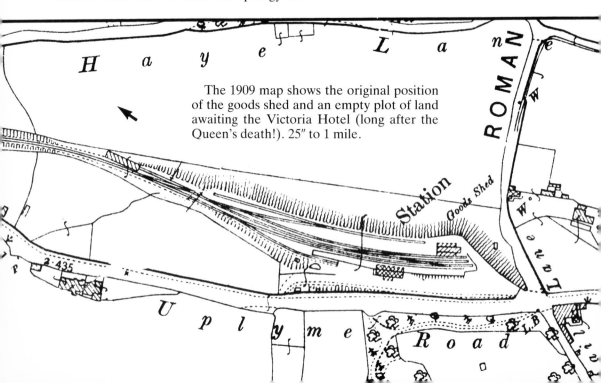

The 1909 map shows the original position of the goods shed and an empty plot of land awaiting the Victoria Hotel (long after the Queen's death!). 25″ to 1 mile.

72. The mace bearer, the mayor and a clergyman in top hat are processing away from the station, behind the representatives of the constabulary. The goods shed was initially much closer to the town and so the station appears in the distance.
(Lyme Regis Museum)

73. A less clear view of the opening train shows it about to return to Axminster, with the locomotive inspector watching a bucket being filled from the injector overflow, no doubt ready for the crew to wash their hands in. No. 734 now survives on the Isle of Wight Steam Railway after a complicated history, described under its original LBSCR no. 46 in our *Branch Line to Hayling*, as it worked on that branch for many years. (British Rail)

74. The Lyme Regis to Axminster horse bus service operated from about 1880 until the opening of the railway. Thereafter, Mr. Groves, its owner, acted as delivery agent for the railway in Lyme, until his death in July 1904. (A.H. Brown collection)

75. Salmon pink coaches stand in the platform prior to the movement of the goods shed, the erection of the Victoria Hotel (few stations could have stood so long without a pub nearby), and the roofing of the gents. Some building work is in progress though. (R.C. Riley collection)

76. An early view of the north and east facades shows the intricate and attractive valance surrounding the building. The *LYME* *REGIS BRANCH* carriage board was carried almost to the end of steam operation. (British Rail)

77. Like the north end, the south appears to have been stripped ready for repainting. Maybe these were official photographs taken when LSWR gained full control of the railway in 1907. (British Rail)

April 1910

AXMINSTER and LYME REGIS.—London and South Western.

Miles	Down. Week Days.	mrn	mrn	aft	aft	aft	aft	aft	aft					
	Axminster.... dep.	8 5	1037	1 7	3 0	4 27	5 50	7 12	8 45	....	....	....	....	....
4¼	Combpyne	8 18	1050	1 20	3 13	4 40	6 3	7 25	8 58	....	....	....	....	....
6¾	Lyme Regis ** arr.	8 25	1057	1 27	3 20	4 47	6 10	7 32	9 5	....	....	....	....	....

Miles	Up. Week Days.	mrn	mrn	mrn	aft	aft	aft	aft	aft	aft				
	Lyme Regis ....dep.	7 12	9b38	9d48	1230	2 20	3 55	4 55	6 30	8 15	....	....	....	....
2½	Combpyne	7 21	9b47	9d57	1239	2 29	4 4	5 4	6 39	8 24	....	....	....	....
6¾	Axminster 120, 123 ar.	7 32	9b58	10d8	1250	2 40	4 15	5 15	6 50	8 35	....	....	....	....

b Fridays only. *d* Except Fridays. ** Station for Charmouth (2 miles).

July 1924

LYME REGIS and AXMINSTER.—Southern

Miles	Up. Week Days only.	mrn	mrn	a	mrn		aft	aft	aft	aft	aft	aft			
	Lyme Regis ......dep.	8 20	9 30	1030	1135	....	1 3	2 3	4 0	5 20	7 15	8 20	....	....	....
2½	Combpyne ....[163	8 29	9 39	1039	1144	....	1 12	2 12	4 9	5 29	7 24	8 29	....	....	....
6¾	Axminster 162, arr.	8 40	9 50	1050	1155	....	1 23	2 23	4 20	5 40	7 35	8 40	....	....	....

NOTES. a Fridays only.

July 1938

AXMINSTER and LYME REGIS.

Miles	Down. Week Days.	SX	SO	mrn	SX	SO	WSX	SO	WO	SX	SX	SO	SX	SO	SX	SO	SX	SO	WSX	aft	aft	
	Axminster..............dep	8 35	8 37	9 39	1042	1128	1232	1246	1248	1 45	2 46	3 16	4 28	4 35	5 38	5 40	6 30	6 58	7 25	8 55	9 40	..
4¼	Combpyne...................	8 47	8 49	9 51	1054	1140	1244	1258	1 0	1 57	2 58	3 30	4 40	4 47	5 50	5 52	6 42	7 10	7 37	9 7	m	..
6¾	Lyme Regis............arr.	8 55	8 57	9 59	11 2	1148	1252	1 6	1 8	2 5	3 6	3 38	4 48	4 55	5 58	6 0	6 50	7 18	7 45	9 15	10 3	..

Down. Sundays.	mrn		mrn		aft	aft		aft		aft		aft		aft		aft		aft		aft		
Axminster..............dep.	1024	..	1116	..	1223	1 48	..	2 45	..	4 30	..	6 0	..	6 54	..	7 58	..	9 5	..	1040	..	..
Combpyne....................	1036	..	1128	..	1235	2 0	..	2 57	..	4 42	..	6 12	..	..	..	8 10	..	9 17	..	1052	..	..
Lyme Regis ....arr.	1044	..	1136	..	1243	2 8	..	3 5	..	4 50	..	6 20	..	7 12	..	8 18	..	9 25	..	11 0	..	..

Miles	Up. Week Days.	mrn	mrn	mrn	mrn	SO	SX	SO		SX	aft	A	SX	B	SX	SO	SX	SO	WSX	WO	aft	
	Lyme Regis............dep.	7 19	8 5	9 10	10 5	1028	1148	1158	..	1 15	2 12	3 45	3 55	4 0	5 5	5 10	6 4	6 15	6 57	7 30	8 22	..
2½	Combpyne....................	m	8 13	9 18	1013	1036	1155	12 6	..	1 23	2 20	3 53	4 3	4 8	5 13	5 18	6 12	6 23	7 5	7 38	8 30	..
6¾	Axminster 342, 348a .. arr.	7 50	8 25	9 30	1025	1048	12 8	1218	..	1 35	2 32	4 5	4 15	4 20	5 25	5 30	6 24	6 35	7 17	7 50	8 42	..

Up. Sundays.	mrn		mrn		mrn		aft		aft		aft		aft		aft		aft		aft		aft		
Lyme Regis ....dep.	9 55	..	1050	..	1150	..	1 8	..	215	..	325	..	532	..	6 27	..	720	..	825	..	9 50	..	..
Combpyne....................	10 3	..	1058	..	1158	..	1 16	..	223	..	333	..	540	..	6 35	..	728	..	833	..	9 58	..	..
Axminster 342, 348a...arr.	1015	..	1110	..	1210	..	1 28	..	235	..	345	..	552	..	6 47	..	740	..	845	..	1010	..	..

A On 24th Sept only B Not after 17th Sept m Southern National Motor Omnibus. Times subject to alteration
SO Sats only SX Sats excepted WO Weds only WSX Weds and Sats excepted

June 1963

AXMINSTER and LYME REGIS

Miles	Down	Mondays to Fridays am	am	am	am	am	pm	pm	pm	pm	pm	pm	pm	pm	pm		Saturdays am	am		am	am	am
	Axminster .. .. dep	7Y40	8 45	9Y55	1032	11Y 5	1233	1 43	2 48	4 21	5 40	6 47	7Y45	8 59	10Y 0	..	7Y40	8 10	..	9 35	1040	11 42
4¼	Combpyne	....	8 56	....	1043	....	1244	1 54	2 59	4 32	5 51	6 58	....	9 10	....	....	....	8 21	....	9 46	1051	11 53
6¾	Lyme Regis .. .. arr	8Y 7	9 3	10Y22	1050	11Y32	1251	2 1	3 6	4 39	5 58	7 5	8Y 8	9 17	10Y27	..	8Y 7	8 28	..	9 53	1058	12 0

Down	Saturdays—continued pm	pm	pm	pm	pm	pm	pm		Sundays am		pm	pm	pm	pm	pm		pm	pm	pm			
Axminster .. .. dep	1243	1K55	4 21	5 42	6 50	8 59	10Y 0	..	11 6	..	1214	1 9	2 30	3 37	4Y55	..	5 48	7 16	8 18	..	..	..
Combpyne	1254	2K 6	4 32	5 53	7 1	9 10	....	....	1117	....	1225	1 20	2 41	3 48	...	....	5 59	7 27	8 29	....	....	....
Lyme Regis .. .. arr	1 1	2K13	4 39	6 0	7 8	9 17	10Y27	..	1124	..	1232	1 27	2 48	3 55	5Y22	..	6 6	7 34	8 36	..	..	..

Miles	Up	Mondays to Fridays am	am	am	am	am	pm	pm	pm	pm	pm	pm		Saturdays am	am		am	am		am		pm
	Lyme Regis .. .. dep	6Y31	7Y21	8 14	9 48	11 39	1 11	2 19	3 46	5 13	6 13	8 29	..	6Y31	7 38	..	8 53	10L13	..	1111	..	12 13
2½	Combpyne	....	....	8 21	9 55	11 46	1 18	2 26	3 53	5 20	6 20	8 36	....	....	7 45	....	9 0	10L20	....	1118	....	12 20
6¾	Axminster .. .. arr	6Y58	7Y48	8 32	10 6	11 57	1 29	2 37	4 4	5 31	6 31	8 47	..	6Y58	7 56	..	9 11	10L31	.	1129	..	12 31

Up	Saturdays—continued pm	pm	pm	pm	pm	pm			Sundays am	am		pm	pm		pm	pm		pm	pm				
Lyme Regis .. .. dep	1 17	3M 8	4Y 1	5 13	6 15	8 29	..	..	1028	1137	..	1240	1 53	..	3 3	5 13	..	6 39	7 47	..	..	..	.
Combpyne	1 24	3M15	....	5 20	6 22	8 36	....	....	1035	1144	....	1247	2 0	....	3 10	5 20	....	6 46	7 54	....	....	....	....
Axminster .. .. arr	1 35	3M26	4Y28	5 31	6 33	8 47	..	..	1046	1155	..	1258	2 11	..	3 21	5 31	..	6 57	8 5	..	..	..	.

K Through Carriages from Waterloo, dep 10 45 am (Table 35). L Through Carriages to Waterloo, arr 1 57 pm (Table 35).
M Through Carriages to Waterloo, arr 6 41 pm (Table 35). Y By Southern National Omnibus between Axminster Station and Lyme Regis. Times subject to alteration

78. In addition to Terrier no. 735 and its set of 4-wheeled coaches, this interesting photograph shows the wooden platform edge with tie bars, the light weight of the original flat-bottomed rail and a single point rod running to the far points. (British Rail)

79. A later view shows the gents to have received a glass roof but the goods shed to still be in its southerly position. In the foreground is the small wooden cattle pen which was replaced by one with concrete posts in the SR era. (Lens of Sutton)

80. The station drive was parallel to the main road, with gates at each end of it. The additional gates on the left must have facilitated the handling of livestock. Note the northern extension of the building, used initially as a bookstall and later as a store. (Lens of Sutton)

81. Few photographs survive of a class 02 on the branch. This is no. 227, one of those 0–4–4Ts that appeared between 1907 and 1914. The superstructure of a breakdown crane appears behind the coaches but we cannot offer an explanation for its presence. The

→

82. The sunblind of the bookstall is up as the sun is setting behind the nameboard which refers to Charmouth. This was more easily reached by bus from Axminster. The specimen rock was no doubt an attraction to visiting geologists but disappeared in a later clear up. (Lens of Sutton)

goods crane was further north and was hand operated, with a capacity of 1¼ tons. (A.H. Brown collection)

LYME REGIS (SR)

83. A view from the down home signal in September 1928 shows the asbestos-clad locomotive shed which replaced a wooden one burnt down on 28th December 1912. The later position of the goods shed is also evident. (Late E. Wallis)

84. A new bookstall was erected at the busier south end of the platform and a gas lamp illuminated an opaque glass bearing the name *W.H. Smith & Son*. This was the station staff in 1928. (A.H. Brown collection)

85. Ex-LBSCR class D1 no. B359 is seen on 4th May 1930, when three other 0–4–2Ts of that class were modified for service on the branch. The bars to protect the windows during coaling were hardly necessary with the cut-down bunkers. (H.C. Casserley)

86. The platform edge was reconstructed in the SR's much-favoured concrete slabs and a new sign omitting Charmouth appeared. Modernised lighting (in gas!) was provided although Lyme had its own hydro-electric plant in a mill in the town centre until after WWII. (H.C. Casserley)

87. By the time this photograph was taken on 29th May 1936, the former bookstall had lost its end windows and served as a useful store. The wooden fence had been supplanted by SR concrete posts with wires. (S.W. Baker)

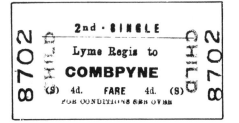

88. An almost timeless scene during the 25 year existence of the SR, although the locomotive displays its non-original Drummond boiler. Coal stands bagged in the yard – as much as 8000 tons were unloaded per annum. (D. Cullum collection)

89. Points to look for, from left to right – a BP tanker between privately owned coal wagons; a horse box (end on); the Victoria Hotel (dangerously sited but never the victim of an accidental over run), and W.H. Smith's bookstall, which was later moved to St. Mary Cray, Kent. (E.R. Lacey collection)

9919

90. A well composed picture shows the double slip in the trackwork which was unusual for a country terminus and more common at large busy stations. It did give flexibility of operation in a layout somewhat restricted in length.(Lens of Sutton)

91. No. 3520 was repainted from green to black in 1941, during the sombre years of WWII. It is seen here in 1947, still in that livery, prior to receiving the number 30584 at the beginning of the following year. (R.C. Riley)

92. The lower quadrant signal and the name board on the front of the signal box were not to last much longer. Rolling stock was migrating widely as an ex-SECR's 'Birdcage' coach arrived in the lengthened bay platform. (Lens of Sutton)

93. One coach usually sufficed in winter but two were used in summer, as witnessed here on 18th September 1947. No. 3488 commenced running on the branch in December 1946, after its long career away from the S.R. (J.H. Aston)

94. Post-war austerity conditions resulted in only one coach being required on the 12.2 pm from Axminster on 28th June 1948. The stretcher cupboard and the glass case for the clock were typical of stations of the period. The renumbering and relettering of locomotives by BR took some time to complete, especially if the shedmaster was nostalgic. (J.H. Aston)

AXMINSTER and LYME REGIS — February 1942

Down	Miles												
		Week Days											
		mrn		mrn		aft	aft	aft		aft	aft	aft	aft
Axminster .... dep		8 35	..	1043	..	1245	1 47	2 47	..	4 33	5 38	6 45	8 55	..
Combpyne	4¼	8 47	..	1055	..	1257	1 59	2 59	..	4 45	5 50	6 57	9 7	..
Lyme Regis .... arr	6¾	8 56	..	11 4	..	1 6	2 8	3 7	..	4 54	5 59	7 6	9 16	..

Down									
			Sundays						
	mrn	aft	aft	aft	aft	aft	aft	aft	
Axminster .... dep	1116	1240	3 0	35	550	7 33	8 30	..
Combpyne	1128	1252	3 12	4 47	6 2	7 45	8 42	..
Lyme Regis .... arr	1137	1 1	3 21	4 56	6 11	7 54	8 51	..

Up	Miles												
		Week Days											
		mrn	mrn	12 9	aft	aft		aft		aft	aft	aft	aft
Lyme Regis .... dep		8 4	..	10 5	12 9	1 14	..	2 13	..	3 55	5 10	6 4	8 21	..
Combpyne	2½	8 12	..	1013	1217	1 22	..	2 21	..	4 3	5 18	6 12	8 29	..
Axminster .... arr	6¾	8 25	..	1026	1230	1 35	..	2 34	..	4 16	5 31	6 25	8 42	..

Up									
			Sundays						
	mrn	mrn	aft	aft	aft	aft	aft		
Lyme Regis .... dep	1045	1142	2 25	4 5	5 10	7 0	7 58	..	..
Combpyne	1053	1150	2 33	4 13	5 18	7 8	8 5	..	..
Axminster .... arr	11 6	12 3	2 46	4 26	5 31	7 21	8 18	..	..

Table 58 — AXMINSTER and LYME REGIS — June 1953

Down	Miles	SO	SX	SO	SO	SX	SO		SX	SO	SX	SO	SX	SO	SX	SO	p.m	p.m	p.m	p.m
Axminster .... dep		8 32	8 35	9 35	1035	1040	11V35	..	12 38	12 45	1 40	1T50	2 50	3 30	4T43	4 43	5 40	6 50	8 55	9V45
Combpyne	6¼	8 44	8 47	9 47	1047	1052	11V47	..	12 45	12 57	1 52	2T23	2	3 32	4T55	4 55	5 52	7 2	9 7	..
Lyme Regis .... arr	6¾	8 53	8 56	9 56	1056	11 1	11V56	..	12 54	1 6	2 1	2T11	3 11	3 41	5T 45	4 6	1T7	11 9	1610V11	

Up	Miles	a.m	SO	SX		SO	SX	SO	SO	SX	SO		SX	SO	SX	SO	p.m	p.m	p.m	p.m
Lyme Regis .... dep		7U15	8 0	8 X	..	9T 0	10 0	10 5	11 5	11T37	12 10	..	1 10	1 22	1 28	2S35	..	3 55	5 10	6 7	8 22
Combpyne	2½		8 8	8 12	..	9T 8	10 8	1013	1113	11T45	12 18	..	1 18	1 20	2 26	2S43	..	4 3	5 18	6 15	8 30
Axminster .... arr	6¾	7U40	8 21	8 25	..	9T21	1021	1026	1126	11T58	12 31	..	1 31	1 33	2 39	2S56	..	4 16	5 31	6 28	8 43

Down			**Sundays**								Up		**Sundays**								
	a.m	p.m	p.m	pm	pm	pm	pm	pm	pm	p.m		a.m	a.m	p.m	pm	pm	pm	p.m	p.m	p.m	p.m
Axminster ... dep	1111	12 6	1 0	223	320	425	550	718	822	923	1025	Lyme Regis .. dep	1040	1137	1233	150	250	355	456	6 45 7	50 8	50 9 50
Combpyne	1123	1218	1 12	236	333	437	6 2	730	835	938	1038	Combpyne	1048	1145	1241	158	258	4 3	5 4	6 53 7	58 8	58 10 8
Lyme Regis ...arr	1132	1227	1 21	244	341	446	611	739	843	946	1046	Axminster ...arr	11 1	1158	1254	211	311	416	517	6 8	11,9	11V1011

B Through Carriages to Waterloo commencing 11th July   **SO** Saturdays only   **SX** Saturdays excepted
T Through Carriages to or from Waterloo   **U** By Southern National Omnibus. Times subject to alteration.
V Through Carriages from Waterloo commencing 4th July

95. The RCTS Special on 28th June 1953, seen earlier at Axminster, was composed of 19th century coaches to add atmosphere, if not comfort, to the occasion. The pilot engine was still no. 30583 for the reverse journey, presumably to help the 0–6–0 round the curves. (P. Hay)

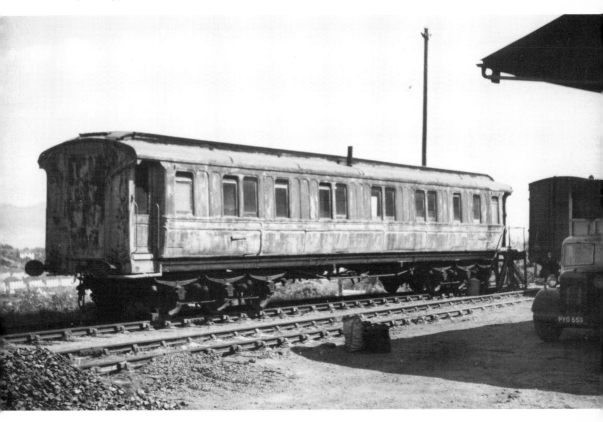

96. A May 1956 view shows that upper quadrant signals had been fitted by then. No. 30582 passes over the dock siding points and clatters past the loco shed. The latter closed on 4th November 1963, upon the withdrawal of steam. (E. Gamblin)

97. Officially named the 'carriage siding', the easternmost siding contained this ex-LNWR twelve-wheeled redundant sleeping car in May 1957. It was used by loco crews overnight at summer weekends. Previously they had to sleep in the goods office! (A.E. Bennett)

98. Modern Bulleid-designed corridor coaches stand in the bay waiting to form a Waterloo service while ageing compartment stock suffices for the local service on 14th July 1957. A railwayman appears to be discussing a coupling problem with the fireman. (P. Hay)

301
SOUTHERN RAILWAY
HALF-DAY EXC'N.
Available as advertised
Waterloo to
LYME REGIS
Third Class

99. The same train departs, devoid of through coaches. Donald King recounts the case of an elderly lady believing that she *was* in a through coach, arriving back at Lyme. A message was sent to Axminster to extract the lady but it was not received by the platform staff and she returned to her starting point yet again! (P. Hay)

100. BR signs are under the gas lamps and BR black lined livery is worn by the locomotives, but otherwise little had changed when this photograph was taken on 3rd July 1958. (J. Scrace)

101. SR uniforms are still evident as the station and footplate staff pose, in 1949. From left to right (back row) S. Bird, R. Huckle, H.A. Frewins, T. Woodman, J. Bull (front row), P. Eveleigh, J. Venton, W.J. Rooks, H. Blanchard and T. Edworthy. (A.H. Brown collection)

102. If a locomotive could look embarrassed, this would have been it. Ex-GWR no. 1462 passes the shed after failing to prove satisfactory on the branch on 12th November 1958. In the background is a permanent way hut and the down home. (S.C. Nash)

103. No. 30583 arrives with the 8.43 from Axminster and reflects the morning sun quite well, on 2nd June 1959. Most main line engines were in a deplorable condition by that time. (J.H. Aston)

104. Nos. 30583 and 30584 double head six coaches up the 1 in 66 gradient, passing under the Uplyme Road bridge, which is on the county boundary. It is the 11.37 am departure on 3rd August 1959. (D. Fereday Glenn)

105. Until the provision of the signal box in 1906 and after its closure on 20th July 1965, the branch was worked on the "one engine in steam" system. The box was similar to the one at Combpyne with 14 levers but only two were spare. To reduce labour, the Tyer's No.6 tablet machine had been moved to the booking office in 1930. (R.C. Riley)

106. At an altitude of 250 ft above sea level, there was usually a good breeze to disperse any excessive smoke. The future Bluebell locomotive departs on 11th August 1959 with a 1921 ex-SECR coach, followed by a corridor coach of 1930 SR construction. (P. Hay)

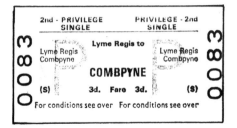

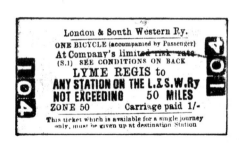

107. Busy summer Saturdays saw double heading of the first down branch train, to bring the relief engine to the terminus. It was uncoupled at the home signal and run into a siding. The train arrived in the bay, as the through coaches would have already been shunted into the platform. The pilot engine would then transfer the branch coaches onto the through ones, thus releasing the other engine, ready to double head back to Axminster. (S.C. Nash)

108. The procedure for shunting incoming goods trains was to stop outside the station, detach the engine (with the coaches, if a mixed train) and gravitate the wagons into the appropriate siding. Apart from bulk traffic such as coal, fertiliser and building materials, general merchandise arrived mixed in vans or sheeted wagons. An exception was a weekly exclusive van for Boots The Chemist, from Beeston, Notts.
(R.C. Riley)

109. Another view of no. 30583 on 14th July 1960 shows that, unlike her sisters, she had only one slide bar each side (also compare pictures 2 and 3). A scene of contrasts – the untidy humble coal staithe; the elegant style of an "Atlantic Tank" and the sheer beauty of the coastline of Lyme Bay. (R.C. Riley)

110. The final view of the clearance test train on 18th September 1960 shows the loading gauge about to be checked against the brake van, which is marked –

TO WORK ON THE
LYME REGIS BRANCH ONLY
NOT IN COMMON USE

It is surprising that this class was introduced so late to the branch and at a time when DMUs were in wide use. (S.C. Nash)

111. The use of class 2s enabled through coaches to be operated for a further three years and for double heading to be eliminated. Their relatively light axle load made them suitable for operation on almost all BR branch lines (R.C. Riley)

112. The Gloucestershire Railway Society appears to have had a new DMU set for its railtour – probably the only one not to have been locomotive hauled. It ran from Cheltenham St. James, via Gloucester Eastgate, Bath Green Park and the Somerset & Dorset line, on 10th May 1958. The return journey was by way of Yeovil, Frome and the North Somerset line. (Lens of Sutton)

113. Regular steam operation ceased on 4th November 1963 but DMU shortage sometimes gave rise to a short reappearance, such as no. 41291 (seen here on 20th February 1965) and an ex-GWR 14XX 0–4–2T with a push-pull set on 15th February 1965. (S.C. Nash)

114. The goods yard, with its continental-style shed, was closed on 3rd February 1964. Here we see unit no. W55000 on 13th March 1965, with the loop retained for emergency use. (C.L. Caddy)

115. Single railcars were introduced in March 1965 and were sometimes insufficient for that final summer peak traffic. No. W555016 stands at the end of the "basic railway" on 8th October 1965. The final few feet of rail were of the original flat bottomed section to the end. (C.L. Caddy)

116. The exterior, on the same day, shows the private road to have been tarmaced at some unrecorded date and the verges and shrubs to have been neglected. Earlier, four licensed taxis operated from this point. (C.L. Caddy)

117. The last day of operation, 27th November 1965, brought enthusiasts of the insane type who lean bodily out of the windows. The athletic type, capable of sitting astride a concrete sign, also came. (C.L. Caddy)

118. Combpyne had a brick-built station with a substantial station master's house in contrast to the minimal timber structure here, devoid of a house. Maybe funds had run low by the time this end of the line was reached. Despite an attempt to preserve the line, the station became neglected. (C. Hall)

119. Buddleias appear to be growing through the broken roof of the boarded up gents while redevelopment plans were discussed. Only recently has the site, which was acquired by the local authority, been developed and now contains a number of small commercial premises. (C. Hall)

Your author, Vic Mitchell, must confess to having had his first branch line encounter as a boy in 1943.

The circumstances were unusual. I spent a large part of my life hiding in dimly lit air-raid shelters from the Luftwaffe who seemed intent on destroying my family and me, instead of the nearby Metropolitan Water Board at Hampton. My main solace was the bulky "Wonder Book of Railways".

Bananas and holidays were something I could not remember and so when my Father announced that we were going to have one week of the latter, explanations were necessary. He told of mines, tank traps and barbed wire covering the beaches of the South Coast with only one known exception – the harbour at Lyme Regis. Reference to the WB of R showed this to be in outer space, in relation to my world.

Arrival at Surbiton station gave me my first sight of main line steam and the start of an unforgettable journey. Innumerable locomotives and endless shunting at Salisbury and Templecombe, but the star in my galaxy was found at Axminster.

The WB of R had been right so far but this beauty had not been included.

Suggestions were made next morning about wet feet and buckets of sand but the lure of the branch was uncontrollable. I have no memory of the harbour but only of frequent footplate trips on no. 3125.

My father had kept one cine film from before the war and was intent on recording the usual beach scenes. In the event, he made a record of the Lyme Regis branch, which I have savoured ever since.

120. Early in 1979, the Mid-Hants Railway removed much of the timber building and later rebuilt it at Alresford, where it once again serves railway passengers, now as a gift and book shop. (Mid-Hants Railway)

There have been many requests for copies of this film when I have shown it at meetings and so I am planning to include it in a video which would also have cine film in colour of my own taking, mostly of branch lines in the South of England, 20 to 25 years ago. In order to gauge demand, a letter expressing interest (and format) could be sent to me at Middleton Press and I will let you know if the idea comes to fruition.

Easebourne Lane, Midhurst, West Sussex, GU29 9AZ
☎ Midhurst (073 081) 3169

BRANCH LINES

BRANCH LINES TO MIDHURST	0 906520 01 0
BRANCH LINES TO HORSHAM	0 906520 02 9
BRANCH LINE TO SELSEY	0 906520 04 5
BRANCH LINES TO EAST GRINSTEAD	0 906520 07 X
BRANCH LINES TO ALTON	0 906520 11 8
BRANCH LINE TO HAYLING	0 906520 12 6
BRANCH LINE TO SOUTHWOLD	0 906520 15 0
BRANCH LINE TO TENTERDEN	0 906520 21 5
BRANCH LINES TO NEWPORT	0 906520 26 6
BRANCH LINES TO TUNBRIDGE WELLS	0 906520 32 0
BRANCH LINE TO SWANAGE	0 906520 33 9
BRANCH LINES AROUND GOSPORT	0 906520 36 3
BRANCH LINES TO LONGMOOR	0 906520 41 X
BRANCH LINE TO LYME REGIS	0 906520 45 2

SOUTH COAST RAILWAYS

BRIGHTON TO WORTHING	0 906520 03 7
WORTHING TO CHICHESTER	0 906520 06 1
CHICHESTER TO PORTSMOUTH	0 906520 14 2
BRIGHTON TO EASTBOURNE	0 906520 16 9
RYDE TO VENTNOR	0 906520 19 3
EASTBOURNE TO HASTINGS	0 906520 27 4
PORTSMOUTH TO SOUTHAMPTON	0 906520 31 2
HASTINGS TO ASHFORD	0 906520 37 1
SOUTHAMPTON TO BOURNEMOUTH	0 906520 42 8

SOUTHERN MAIN LINES

WOKING TO PORTSMOUTH	0 906520 25 8
HAYWARDS HEATH TO SEAFORD	0 906520 28 2
EPSOM TO HORSHAM	0 906520 30 4
CRAWLEY TO LITTLEHAMPTON	0 906520 34 7
THREE BRIDGES TO BRIGHTON	0 906520 35 5
WATERLOO TO WOKING	0 906520 38 X
VICTORIA TO EAST CROYDON	0 906520 40 1
TONBRIDGE TO HASTINGS	0 906520 44 4

STEAMING THROUGH

STEAMING THROUGH KENT	0 906520 13 4
STEAMING THROUGH EAST HANTS	0 906520 18 5
STEAMING THROUGH EAST SUSSEX	0 906520 22 3
STEAMING THROUGH SURREY	0 906520 39 8

OTHER RAILWAY BOOKS

WAR ON THE LINE The official history of the SR in World War II	0 906520 10 X
GARRAWAY FATHER AND SON The story of two careers in steam	0 906520 20 7